Polished Stones

A POETRY COLLECTION

by

Cynthia Schumacher

the Peppertree Press

Sarasota, Florida

ISBN: 978-1-61493-516-2
Library of Congress Number: 2017905723
Printed April 2017

For Nina

United in faith and friendship

Other books by the author:

Poetry Collections
Firefly Encounters
Wellspring Legacies
Soul Candles
Creekstone Crossings
Seeds from Wild Grasses

Books for Children
Colorful Character
Searching for S
Willenbron and the Gralumpy
Fairytale Musical for Children
Rapunzel

Contents

EXPLORING

HUMOR

COMMEMORATION

Exploring

Private Collection

The people found throughout the years
who have the greatest influence on one's life
are like a priceless cache of lodestars
and small polished stones, preserved within
the velvet folds of memory for later contemplation.
Some were but briefly known yet unforgettable,
still able to rekindle sparks of comradeship
and inner strength in trying times.
Others had larger, more demanding roles,
serving as visionary guides toward goals
that seemed at first to be impossible.
For one who honors these enduring gifts
of humankind, no sincere sense of gratitude
can ever be enough. True merit lies
with living so as to become a worthwhile part
of someone else's treasure trove.

Scenic Interludes

1

St. Patrick's Day announces spring.
Crape myrtle trees wear tiny beads
of leaf buds on their stems,
shrub roses bloom,
and in one garden bed
clusters of daylilies,
renouncing dormancy,
are flourishing thick bushy clumps
of leaves that look like shaggy tops
of green-haired Irish gnomes
emerging from the soil.

2

In this parched place of
bleached rock and swirling sand
pink cactus flowers bloom.
Tumbleweeds are loose,
bouncing about like wiry knots
of hair torn from the heads
of battling giants.
Eagle soars, dives, wheels,
streaks away, swerves back and forth,
building air castles.

3

In later years one feels time flow
inexorably, impersonally, and
usually imperceptibly
until the fragile moments
when it seems to slow
for one to see
the crystal globes of dew
balance upon a leaf
or dogwood petals ride the wind
like small white butterflies.

Time's a Traveler

Time's a traveler —
the worst kind.
Never stops
to let you find
if he's someone
nice to know,
if he's either
friend or foe.
Best you smile
and catch his eye
so he'll wave
when passing by.

Optimist's Gamble

Who can be sure of what life will bring?
We tend to assume as days come and go
that during some hours the sun will shine
or clouds will converge for the rain to fall,
that a magical moment or terrible time
will arrive and depart like the ocean's flow,
that even when feeling we're most secure,
the chance is still present we're not at all.
Should we yield to uncertainty, steep in despair,
and rail against heaven for placing us there?
Beyond each dark passage lie embryo dreams,
spurring goals worth pursuing and songs to be sung,
rich with triumphs to cherish and bells to be rung.
A leaf on a branch cannot glimpse the whole tree,
so how can we learn what our future will be
unless we believe we have one?

Visitor

A leprechaun's in my garden.
He doesn't think I know,
but from my morning window
I see him come and go.
He dances through the daisies
to make the pansies smile
and nods at amaryllis blooms
dressed in high fashion style.
The bean plants in the garden
grow faster than before,
and berry branches indicate
this year I'll harvest more.

I have no wish to capture him.
He's done no mischief here.
Perhaps he's just an aging elf
who wants to bring me cheer
before he disappears one day
to where such creatures go
when summer ends and fall winds rise
to warn of winter snow.
No pot of riches will I seek.
Instead I'll leave him free
to later cloak with flowers of gold
my tabebuia tree.

Centenarian

On the party day at the nursing home
to which the family came, four generations strong,
she sat at a table bright with colored bows,
under a silver and green banner,
in front of a giant cake
topped with a large white rose
and little yellow birds ready to sing.
Uncertain what all the fuss was about
because of so much chatter from the throng,
she heard someone ask a question and realized
that everyone seemed to be looking at her.
"How does it feel to be 100 years old, dear?"
It was then she became aware
of the large pink balloon
tied with a string to an extra chair,
and she remembered the day she had gone
to Atlantic City with her father,
where he had bought her a bag of salt water taffy
on her tenth birthday.
She knew exactly what that felt like;
so she replied to this puzzling inquiry
in the polite manner she had been taught as a child
to respond to an important question to which
she did not really know the answer,
"I have no idea."

Insomnia

The restless mind spurns slumber.
Throughout the endless night
it prowls about on soft-shod feet,
seeking the clear-eyed sanity
of dawn.

Transformation

The meadow woke one morning,
pre-programmed for surprise,
and in the time that followed
it changed before my eyes.
The great expanse of arid grass
was startled into green
to promise springtime's entrance
would verge on the extreme.
Soon multitudes of daffodils
advanced in waves of gold,
attended by wild iris, asters too,
and in the shaded spots beside a stream
small violets and tall cardinal flowers grew.

The sweep of color stretching far
delighted mind and gaze,
inviting possibilities
of outdoor ramble days.
A sudden realization came
that in this visual feast
of countless blades and blossoms
no single thing was least
among the many others
now dwelling in this place.

Each was uniquely fashioned
to form the lovely face
of Nature's primal majesty and grace,
innumerable perfections into one.

Summer Sight

Along the far side of the garden,
rising above and beyond
asters and daylilies,
pentas and coneflowers,
competing for color accolades,
they stand serene, imposing,
impeccably arrayed in green and yellow,
gigantic one-eyed sentinels
on the perimeter of a parade—
sunflowers!

Recurrence

Returning to a house in which you lived
when you were young is thought by some to have
one rite-of-passage, universal theme:
you come, you find it, yet it's not the same.
It's true. After a space of many years
I have returned to see this place again.
Immediately I feel the stab of loss.
The house, two-storied on its corner lot,
seems different as though the outer walls
have shrunk, contracted into smaller space.
The yard displays neglect. The ancient oaks
are burdened with gray moss, and shrubs unpruned
struggle to live among invasive weeds.
No red hibiscus nods beside the porch.
The poinciana tree that in the spring
unfurled a canopy of yellow blooms
is gone. Only the remnant of its rotted stump
remains. The attic window where I viewed,
as from a castle tower, the pulsing flow
of people's lives in networked neighborhoods
is blank and empty underneath the eaves.
No longer does it frame a youthful form
that often gazed upon this changing scene
and dreamed of destinies not yet fulfilled.

I see it all and harbor no regrets
for places cannot hoard our memories.
Just as we're told words have no meaning
in and of themselves,
so do all memory meanings live in us.
We always own the power to find
if what we've long remembered still exists
to bring us home again.

At Random

Viewed through a sunlit window,
the double helix
suspended in the garden
turns and twirls and whirls.
The eye records;
the left brain ascertains
the wind is blowing;
the right brain enters timeless space
and contemplates
how seamlessly the energy that flows
from heaven and earth
is blended beyond sight and sound,
teaching the mind that all is one.

Amphibian Tourist Attraction

plop...
plop...
plop...
It's very close now — just ahead
on Royal Pond, beside a mossy bank
where trillium and wild iris grow
beneath an ancient tree.
A few hops more and you'll soon see
the place where he once lived
until that transformational day.
Stop by. You'll find it worth the time.
He's famous now, of course,
but evidence remains
of what he used to be.
Look for a weather-beaten sign that reads:

His Excellency Francisco Frog
Friend and Protector
100 Lily Pad Lane
Wild Kingdom Bog
Travelers Welcome
Special Accommodations for Princesses

Grace

A love that lasts forever is not found
in episodes of popular acclaim
where trust and true commitment are not bound
to undergird the risks of sudden fame.
Nor will it be in splendor's gleaming walls
of luxury where power and wealth reside,
shouting their worth as greater than the calls
for help from those with needs who wait outside.
Such love arrives in less expected ways —
in times of doubt when hope and faith seem gone,
in circumstances plagued by troubled days
and dark night fears that whisper until dawn.
Then can it come, if asked, to let us know
we're never lost if we but say hello.

Query

Can you make a good dream vanish?
It will find a way to grow.
It will find a way to flower
in the midst of ice and snow.
It will search and pause and linger
where ideas ebb and flow
in the lives of people seeking
to escape from lives of woe.
You can try to stop the dreamers
to make sure they won't survive,
but the dreams will just lie waiting
for another chance to thrive.
If we want tomorrow's children
to enjoy a different day
where endless opportunities
are revealed in vast array,
we must always keep believing
that good dreams will never die,
for they can reshape the future
when the ones who dream them try.
Can you make a good dream vanish
so it cannot ever grow?
For a while, one can contain it,
but ultimately, no.

Ninety-five and Counting

When you were eighty-eight, we celebrated,
delighted that you'd come so far
and would soon reach your ninetieth year.
Of course, you passed that splendid mark
so easily we barely noticed it was gone,
and so we pause to celebrate again.
Hooray! You've added five years more!
No matter what occurs you choose to thrive
to share your insights and wise points of view
within our motley band of bibliophiles.
So even if in days ahead
you need to travel on in different style,
in wagon motorized, in favorite chair
with wheels attached, in rickshaw
powered by magic roller skates,
no matter what it takes
to get you closer to a century,
we'll tie a long rope to the back
and hang on for the ride.

Celebration Song

She was always for us a person of distinction.
Her quest for knowledge was remarkable,
her love for family and friends a constant gift.
Throughout the years she influenced others
to think more deeply and to strive
for pinnacles of excellence in their lives.
Toward the end she seemed to be
sheathed in an ancient fabric,
fine and tissue-thin, whose fragile threads
might fray and separate at any time,
but woven through and intertwined
with filaments of spiderweb,
their tensile strength so strong
all held until her 97th year.
Now she is gone, drifting away,
like gentle ripples on a pond
until the surface flattens and is still.
We miss her presence here.
We always will.

Questing

When contemplating pros and cons
of immortality, of whether God exists,
of whether true reality extends beyond the grave,
the mind sometimes retreats,
now overpowered by uncertainty,
by inability to comprehend
how peaks of ecstasy and joy
could ever be sustained at will.
It topples into wells of unbelief:
the afterlife is just a myth; there's nothing more;
we die and that's the end of everything.
Before our birth, when in the womb
where we felt safe and warm,
we had no conscious inkling of another world
until urged forth. We came, a separated form,
exposed to hot and cold and visibility.
Accommodating to this different state,
the memories of where we'd been,
if any did remain, were formless, fading,
and would disappear.
In time we grew more comfortable,
and on this earth we never had envisioned,
it seemed we'd reached our final destination.
Yet as we age, among us live

so many who imagine more to come.
Though often called deluded,
the victims of a foolish, storied lore,
they still believe.
For them this search for closure is a gift,
a seeking of the meditating soul
which animates the body, dwells unseen,
alert to insights of divinity encompassing
this little bubble of the natural world
until we die, and then it travels on
beyond the womb of time
directly to its uncreated Source
where it is sheltered by an infinite grace
and destined to rejoin its former shell,
transfigured in eternity.

Child Lessened

Some people think when death arrives,
he wears a frightful face.
They say he's like a monster
who comes from outer space.

My mother died when I was four.
They said she flew away.
I used to think that she was lost
and had no place to stay,

but now she visits me in dreams
and tells me not to fear.
This is a lovely land, she says,
I'm very happy here.

I think death's like a window blind
that filters out the sun,
that when you open it, you see
a place to have great fun.

I don't know how long I will live,
but when it's time to die,
I hope my mother brings me wings
and teaches me to fly.

Untitled...

Tonight the yellow
blooms of poinciana tree
are moonlight-silvered.

Puzzled Pilgrim

Death they call it. What's it like?
If I met it, would I feel it?
Would I know it if it happened?
Ponder this analogy:
two of us on different trains,
each train idling in the station,
side by side with nothing moving.
One train moves, the other stays.
Am I sure which pulled away?
One of us might live in time
and another timeless be.
Would we know which one is gone,
or would the timeless one believe
he was present still and free,
capable to travel on?
Might there be another station
where each of us found the other,
where we suddenly discover
we are riding the same train,
something we cannot explain?
As these questions swirl around,
answers yet I have not found.
It's quite likely heaven knows.
Death has no opinion.

Anniversary Introspective

Was it the comfortable warmth of her smile
or the pleasure he sensed in her gaze?
Was it discovering the values he shared
or his leisurely, soft-spoken ways?
Whatever the reason, something connected
and thus the course of their lives was affected.
Now with the time that has passed in between,
they've arrived at this yearstone for others to see
how mutual attraction has helped them pursue
complementary life ventures, with each of them free
to flourish together or flourish apart,
while deeper connections grow slowly unseen,
nurtured wisely by love and enshrined in the heart.

Fall Favorite

Of all the trees that bring us autumn leaves,
I love the maple near my garden wall the best.
Enhancing its spectacular appeal,
it graciously allows among its boughs
some branches from a nearby sweet gum tree
to intersperse themselves.
No simple green to yellow change like poplars do
or dogwood-quick conversions to an Indian red,
but rather wild diversity is clearly maple's quest:
masses of creamy yellow here and there,
bright orange and amber too, melon and gold
and sudden scarlet swirls, along with leaves,
still summer green, deciding what to do —
all mixed together everywhere. And as
this riotous color steals the scene, to all
its fluttering flock the maple seems to say:
You know you must eventually turn brown,
but while you have the chance,
wear all your colors splendidly, and when
winds turn you loose and whirl you through the air,
fly high and join the dance.

Brief Encounter

Long ago when life seemed dull,
there came a certain summer day
which changed his listless mood because
Amanda Figlet danced his way.

She danced across a boxwood hedge.
She danced around a maple tree.
She danced right through his open gate
and said, Come down and dance with me.

He sputtered lamely; she just laughed
and told him it was time to play.
She danced up steps to where he sat.
She seized his hand. They danced away.

They danced down streets and into parks.
She twirled and spun him round and round.
They leaped and leaned and bowed and pranced.
His feet could barely touch the ground.

Why are you doing this? he gasped.
Where are we going, crazy girl?
Just dance, my darling, she replied.
Just dance and let the world unfurl.

And so they danced across the hills
and over meadows broad and green,
and as they danced, she taught him how
to see more keenly, laugh, and dream.

And at the last in sun and rain,
they danced to celebrate the day,
and then she danced him home again.
Have fun! she said and danced away.

So many years have passed since then,
and now he welcomes every day,
no matter what its choices bring,
because Amanda danced his way.

Sage Advice

Hold any of these in your hand —
the future of a family,
the life of an individual,
the trust of a child,
the integrity of a promise,
the power of an idea,
the destiny of a nation.
Whatever you become,
whatever you do,
make wise decisions.
Everything in life harbors an unsuspected fragility.

Visiting Melchior

Yes, I am he. The other two are gone,
and I remain, now wondering why I've been allowed
to reach this pinnacle, my ninety-second year.
Well, God is good. He lets me feel my age
yet keep my memories, the ones I value most.

Tonight I walked outside to sit beneath the sky
and search for slender ribbons of breeze.
I like this time before full darkness comes
when stars remain concealed behind the veil of dusk.
Soon one will venture forth, an ordinary star of course,
just bright enough to wake the past and celebrate
nights of exceptional brilliance long ago.

More than a year we traveled then to find
that modest house. What was our visit like?
Far different than we ever could imagine.
The house was small, well-built, with a workspace
along one side because the husband was
a carpenter. His wife was young and comely,
her manner graceful and serene.
And the child … a sturdy little boy just past the age of one,
who stood at first within the circle of his mother's arm
and watched us shyly as we introduced ourselves.

We brought forth gifts, among which were
three jeweled boxes filled with precious things
and a fine rug woven in Babylon.
The couple stared in wonder as we spoke
and thanked us gravely afterward, unsure
what more to say. To break an awkward silence
we spread the rug upon the floor
and asked to sit with them as friends
to share some details of our lives
and better come to know the child.
They rushed to make us comfortable then,
to bring us fresh-baked bread and wine.

We sat together thus, talking about our travels,
describing our years of studying the heavens
and words in ancient manuscripts.
There came a moment when we shared with them
our private names, the ones familiar to our friends,
and as we did, the boy left his place
beside his mother and capered about,
trying to speak the names we called ourselves.
At first he ran to Bal to feel his mustache
and his long black beard, a fearsome mass
of tangled, fuzzy curls. Next he moved on
to Kasper to twirl the golden tassels
fringing the collar of his silken shirt
and the ends of his voluminous sleeves.

And then he came to me.
He pointed to the polished stone that hung
from a leather thong around my neck,
a small white stone discovered in a riverbed
by my only son when he was five years old.
I found it later in his box of treasured objects
after his death at twenty-three when rocks
upon a cliffside crumbled beneath his feet
and he fell into shadows far below.
I'd worn it ever since to match the stony sheath
that anger formed around my heart that day.
That moment when the boy approached
and looked at me—I had no words to say.
How could I speak of death to this young child
or of the bitterness a grieving parent feels?
As it happened, I did not have to speak at all,
for suddenly the boy laughed and climbed into my lap.
He touched the stone and tried to say my name.
"Melk, Melk," he chanted, putting his arms
around my neck, kissing my cheek.
"Melk, Melk," he babbled happily again,
then climbed back down and danced away
to sit between his parents on the rug
and chew a crust of bread contentedly.
During our later journey home, using a different route,
the three of us discussed at length that day.
What had we found that indicated royalty?

How strange we must have looked,
entering that humble home in our fine robes,
bringing those lavish gifts to a small child
with beautiful eyes who looked so ordinary otherwise.
And yet we all agreed we'd sensed
a radiant richness that could not be explained.
I wonder, did that boy indeed become a king
in later years as all our calculations showed
would come to pass? I'll never know.
He would be in his thirties now, a man mature,
but it's unlikely I'll live long enough
for news of that far land to come my way.
Ah well, perhaps he did become a king,
one of a different kind — a monarch who
would govern wisely, concerned with human hearts
and minds rather than with great wealth and power.
One thing I know.
The moment that the boy touched the stone I wore
and put his arms around me,
that hardened covering inside my chest dissolved,
and then I felt my son come back to me.

Nikwasi Mound 2016

Throughout the day upon a city lot,
within the sounds and sights of streets and stores,
it stands alone.
Although its height is less imposing now,
it still reminds the passersby
that it exists because in recent decades
its legacy was recognized, its visibility
preserved from transitory fame.
Once central as a busy place for trade,
it waits in silence now for something to occur
to reconnect its past to present day,
perhaps by local folk committed to
wise use of Nature's realm.
Indeed this reconnection already may be near
as new green spaces here and there restored
move closer to this sacred site.
It well may be when future generations come
to view these areas naturally reclaimed
as links to ancient history,
that some who are intuitively inclined
may feel a sudden shifting in the air,
a sense of kindred closeness,
as though the spirits of those tribes
who flourished here

throughout a thousand years or more —
the Pisgah and the Cherokee,
the Nunne'hi warriors in their battle dress —
are now alert, moving about unseen
among their modern visitors,
to share their friendship and protection
and welcome all to join in this
millennial reunion.

Life Companion

Walk with me when the dawn is new
when the sunlight burnishes leaves of spring
and the daffodils wear jewels of dew.

Work with me through the busy day
where the tasks of the world need many hands
and we have a vital part to play.

Sit with me in the sunset hours
as life flows by at a slower pace,
as thoughts roam free and reflection flowers.

Rest at last when the night arrives,
linked by the love that friendship brings,
blessed by the peace that God provides.

Humor

Limerick O'Malley

A chatty old broad named O'Malley
was found lying drunk in an alley.
When asked how she got
to this miserable spot,
she slurred, "On a comet named Halley."

Limerick LaRue

There once was a girl named LaRue
who could seldom decide what to do.
When caught in a blizzard,
she dithered and shivered
till she froze to a popsicle blue.

Her fur-coated lover named Warmes,
a fellow of multiple charms,
came and said, "Dear LaRue,
I know just what to do.
When I hug you, you'll melt in my arms."

Reversal

Melinda McRee was the chatterbox queen.
On social occasions her reign was supreme.
No topic was mentioned that she could resist.
Once comments began she would quickly insist
that everyone hear what she wanted to say,
and then she would talk for the rest of the day,
no matter who happened to be within range,
no matter how often the subject would change.
Family who cared said, "We want her to thrive,
but by constantly talking she'll never survive.
She may want to marry. She's pretty and smart,
but talking too much could make boyfriends depart.
She's just so annoying, yet what can we do?"
So they fretted until entered Angus McGrew,
a wealthy young banker, then seeking a wife,
who sought her attention and altered her life.
Though a man of few words, he called her most charming.
She responded demurely, which to him was disarming.
Listening at length to what else he might say,
she began to converse in a quite normal way.
(With those of few words you must listen a lot
or else you can't share in the things they have thought.)
In time they were married, a happy event,
and all proclaimed Angus to be heaven-sent.

Yet Angus was not only loving but wise,
for he knew that his wife had a talent to prize.
He allowed her to manage the bank that he owned,
so when gangs tried to rob it, they afterward groaned,
"We gave up because of that woman inside
who talked us to death about violence and sin
and lost chances in life till we finally gave in.
She said she could teach us new ways to make money
so we could have lives which were crime-free and sunny.
She said she would help us if we were indicted.
It sounded so great we got really excited!"
So the end of this story is truly quite clear:
A habit that hobbles may someday endear
and be something of value when love enters in
and changes one greatly from what one has been.

Limerick Randy

A fat little guy known as Randy
craved attention in any way handy.
Dressed in stripes white and red,
he would shout it was said,
"Look at me! I'm a peppermint dandy!"

Limerick Darrell

A drunken young rowdy called Darrell
found himself in considerable peril
in an old country store
where he staggered and swore
and fell into brine in a barrel.

Commemoration

"First Advent" and "Ash Wednesday" first appeared
in my earlier collection *Soul Candles,* published in 1998.

First Advent

Out of the darkness, radiance;
out of the silence, singing…
Here is a time when journeying does not tire us.
Amazement yields to unexpected joy.
Traveling across the hills,
drawn toward a place unknown unless in dreams,
we do not mind how far.
Our eyes are fixed upon the star.
Around us in the gentle night
we feel a tangible serenity; we share
a fellowship of soaring, sheltering wings.
We walk and are content in a surfeit of angels.

Advent Passing

At this time,
whether the wind rises,
moaning insistently before the dawn,
or gently lifts the leaves of sleeping trees,
whether the moon is full as it floats by
or absent from a sky profuse with stars,
watch; listen.
Perhaps there will be singing in the night;
perhaps in homes on city streets
and down the country lanes
small, colored lights will bloom
and shimmer without sound;
and later on perhaps a hush will fall
and spread across the darkened land
as if to sense what none can truly see or hear
but only feel—
Love's presence near,
Love's presence all around.

Safe Harbor

How deceptive it is near the close of the year
to be caught in the flow of a seasonal tide
of searching for gifts and trimming a tree,
or dealing with traffic and places to go,
of riding at night through the neighborhoods
to view spectacular light displays
and windows softened by candle glow;
but if you long for what often seems lost,
the original reason to celebrate,
alter your course toward an earlier time
where, wonderstruck, you can contemplate
a brave young girl and a trusting spouse,
angelic voices high above
in the dazzling light of a single star,
and a Child whose promise is infinite love.
If with this vision you choose to stay,
you truly can welcome Christmas Day.

Silent Night

After the fatigue of traveling far,
after the birth,
as all around her earth grew still
and time moved slowly on
in the hours before the dawn,
she fell asleep,
curled up against a mound of straw,
a small cloth resting underneath her cheek,
placed there to ease the roughness of the grain,
while the child, wide awake,
lying comfortable and safe
in the bend of her arm,
gazed into the night with new bright eyes
and contemplated his arrival inside Creation.

Holy Night

Across the neighborhood the stillness reigns.
No cars pass by. The gentle wind
of early evening which seemed to promise rain
has died some hours ago, clouds drift away,
and now the heavens are overwhelmed with stars.
The festive decorations glittering in the yards,
as if aware they are no competition for the brilliance
of the sky, wink out when timer-prompted,
leaving homes barely visible beneath the trees.
With midnight past, time moves into those alien hours
when darkness seems to have no end.
Advent departs and Christmas Day, unheralded
by those asleep, arrives and waits to bring
the miracle of sunlight with the dawn.
For children it can never come too soon.
For those of greatest age it offers hope
to have the blessing of another year.

Invitation to the Dance

When faced with turbulent times,
perspective can be lost as honesty
and reasoned discourse are replaced
with fraud and incivility.
The ancient sages say:
To every front there is a back.
Thus it is well to be reflective.
Good people die when nature's fury rules,
but afterward survivors meet with strangers
arrived from foreign lands to offer aid.
A noble cause does not succeed,
yet from the ashes of defeat
friendships that otherwise would not have been
are forged and long endure.
In optimism lies the chance
to counterbalance bad with good.
Now is the season to repair
the views of cynical philosophers.
The scent of pine is in the air,
and candle glow is once again in style.

Christmas

On this memorable night,
the stars thickly clustered overhead,
unfettered and self-igniting,
born in the beginning before recorded time,
are reminders of the miracle of Light,
the gift which makes possible
man's ability to discern such disparate things
as the shape of shadows,
the brilliant colors blooming on cavern walls,
and the genetic affinity of humanity
for illumination.
Thus do we celebrate and respond
to this marvelous sight
with the friendly glow of lanterns and candles,
the endless blaze and glitter of city thoroughfares,
the traveling cloudbursts of radiance
winding their way
through shrubbery and along rooftops
as visible revelations of
a universal connection to Life.

Full Circle

In those who have received the gift of faith
belief is strong that God has always loved
the world. Yet when one studies distant centuries,
old writings tend to tell of man's iniquity
and God's severe response.
Amid such wrongful acts and cataclysmic happenings
the quiet voice of heavenly grace
would sometimes go unheard or be ignored.
Forgotten was the boundless love
that fashioned Adam, for it also left men free
to disobey as well as praise their Maker.
Blessed are we who live in later times
and see God's love so differently revealed.
A trusting woman gave consent and He was born,
the Son of God, an infant vulnerable, of lowly state,
and kin to all mankind —
this brings the ancient message home.
Each Christmas season when believers celebrate
and sense the hope that new beginnings bring,
both young and old unite to pray for peace
and sing with joy because God's love endures,
made visible in every child.

Variations on a Timely Theme

It comes again—
for some, a season cherished and defined
by revelry and decorated homes,
bright colors, family gatherings,
hundreds of twinkling lights and carols sung.

For others, often overwhelmed by age
and personal adversity,
it may project an absence of enthusiasm,
feelings of loneliness and loss,
or cynical unwillingness to welcome joy.

And yet, among so many can be found
people in whom the gift of faith resides,
where intuition is allowed to have its say.
They sense connections everywhere.
They ponder links between the atoms
of snowmen melting in the yard
and those of mighty waters born in ancient seas
that flow together all around the earth.
They see the trees with amputated feet
for sale in city lots and wonder
if their branches tingle with delight
when touched by human hands,
warm with the energy all life contains.

They feel their kinship to the homeless man
who finds discarded scraps of tinsel
in a garbage can and hangs them on the rusty rims
of his donated shopping cart
in memory of better days.

When rains come later in the winter night
and high winds vibrate over house and hill,
the little girl who wakens feels no fear,
for she believes the sounds
are but the cosmic rush of massive angel wings,
spreading to shelter all that lies below,
present to herald the Child reborn each year
in hearts and minds of those who understand
what Christmas means.

Text Message/Timeless

In the worst of times
when selfish acts abound
to make it seem
that kindness is an aberration,
some live among us,
choice and circumstance
having shaped their lives
to show respect for all,
to persevere in helping others see
reflections of God's love.
They continue to care,
these ordinary souls
who have sampled the wine
of wisdom and found it good.
They are always here,
working in quiet ways,
perhaps unrecognized for years,
bringing to those in need
the seeds of hope
and the sunlight of joy.

Ash Wednesday

Under low clouds,
thick-rolled like gray sausages,
oak leaves lie in sodden heaps on the grass
till the dry wind comes;
then they lift renewed,
light and crisp,
chattering and whirligigging over rooftops,
spinning in brown spirals to ground again.
The fine black grains of palm ashes mark us.
We walk with the shadow of death on our foreheads
and contemplate our proximity to ancestral dust.
The land, rough-barked and dun-colored,
slumbers in the sheath of winter.
But there are tiny green tips
on the fig branches,
and soon the sunbeam children
will rise with the morning and sing.

Easter

Past midnight
when the day began,
long before morning sun,
hours before the women came
and saw and ran,
that instant when
no one was there to see
the resurrected form appear
in its solidity,
able to pass
through unsubstantial walls
of cave and stone and olive tree,
then was it really true,
the dawning of the kingdom promised,
our way to God exalted, new.

Dawnsong

Awake, awake, the night is done.
Awake, awake, the sun is come.
This is the moment when we pray:
May God be with us through this day.

Author's Afterword

Occasionally I have heard people say they do not like to read modern poetry because they do not understand it or because it doesn't rhyme like "old-fashioned" poetry used to do. My response has usually been to mention that anyone writing poetry today is a modern poet and heir to all forms and styles of poetry ever discovered. An author is thereby free to use any examples available from past or present years to influence his work. If rhyme or meter dominate a certain poem or if unrhymed, unmetered free verse is evident instead, this really should matter only to the writer who has decided this is absolutely the only way he can be satisfied the poem should exist.

I have always believed that poetry can be described as "word music" and that certain poems just like certain kinds of music will appeal to various individuals more than to others. A poem's shape, structure, choice of words, possible meaning, etc. may be unique to its author, but when it produces some favorable response, whether personal or universal in readers, it may eventually grow in its appeal to a wider audience for different reasons in later times. My own experiences in becoming familiar with the poetry of writers throughout history have influenced me to explore writing poems in a variety of ways, often causing diverse individuals who are usually reluctant to reading any poetry to select certain poems as their favorites.

The desire to share one's seemingly inexpressible thoughts completely and clearly in written form with another human being is a perilous endeavor and often unsuccessful. Perhaps the intricate and frustrating process of determining the best words to use in writing a poem worth saving is the closest one can come to achieving this crossover.

 Cynthia Schumacher is a retired public school teacher who has served in later years as a part-time K-12 educational consultant on constructive approaches to teaching and learning. A native of Florida, she has lived in Lake County during most of her career and resides now in Sebring where she continues to be active in community and church affairs. In her poetry talks before clubs, educational organizations and a variety of other small groups, she is recognized for her enjoyable presentations on the connection between poetry and human experience.

9 781614 935162